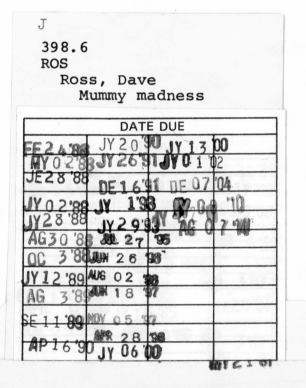

MUMMY MADNESS

half-title
page

MUMMY MADNESS

JOKES RIDDLES THINGS TO DO
BY
DAVE ROSS

FRANKLIN WATTS NEW YORK LONDON 1979
TORONTO

FOR EDDY & JOEL

Library of Congress Cataloging in Publication Data

Ross, David, 1949-
Mummy madness.

SUMMARY: Puns, riddles, jokes, and things to do,
all featuring mummies.
1. Riddles—Juvenile literature. 2. Mummies—Anecdotes, facetiae, satire, etc. 3. Wit and humor—
Juvenile. [1. Mummies—Anecdotes, facetiae, satire,
etc. 2. Jokes. 3. Riddles] I. Title.
PN6371.5.R66   398.6   79-13494
ISBN 0-531-04094-1

HOW CAN YOU CATCH A MUMMY?

HIDE BEHIND A SAND DUNE AND MAKE A NOISE LIKE A PYRAMID.

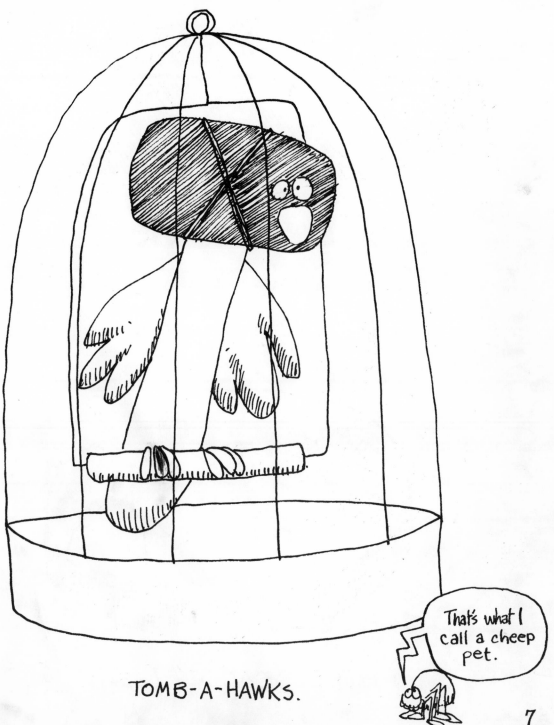

TOMB-A-HAWKS.

A MUMMY SUITCASE

THE DEAD "C" (SEA)

EASY-TO-BUILD PYRAMID

WHAT YOU WILL NEED

A LARGE CARDBOARD BOX
SOMEONE TO CUT THE CARDBOARD
A RULER
TAPE
A CRAYON OR MARKER

WHAT TO DO

① CUT THE BOX ALONG THE
   SIDES AND MAKE FOUR SQUARES
② MEASURE AND MARK OUT A
   TRIANGLE THAT FILLS THE SQUARE
③ CUT OUT THE TRIANGLE AND USE
   IT TO TRACE THREE OTHERS
④ CUT OUT THE LAST THREE TRIANGLES
   AND TAPE TOGETHER
⑤ DRAW A STONE BLOCK PATTERN

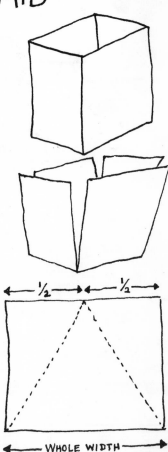

½ — ½

WHOLE WIDTH

OTHER IDEAS

PAINT ON A COAT OF WHITE GLUE
AND SPRINKLE WITH SAND
            OR
USE THE PYRAMID AS A FORM AND
COVER THE OUTSIDE WITH SUGAR CUBES

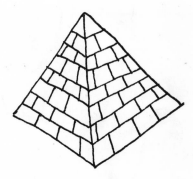

9

THIS IS MORTIMER AND HIS PET SNAKE, ASP.

MORTIMER IS SO DUMB HE THINKS THE JEWELS IN A MUMMY'S TREASURE ARE CALLED TOMBSTONES.

WHAT DID THE MUMMY SAY TO HIS VICTIM?

ITS BEEN NICE GNAWING YOU.

WHAT WAS THE MUMMY'S FAVORITE PAINTING?

WHISTLER'S MUMMY.

14

WHY DID THE LITTLE MUMMY GET HIS MOUTH WASHED OUT?

HE SAID A MUMMY'S CURSE.

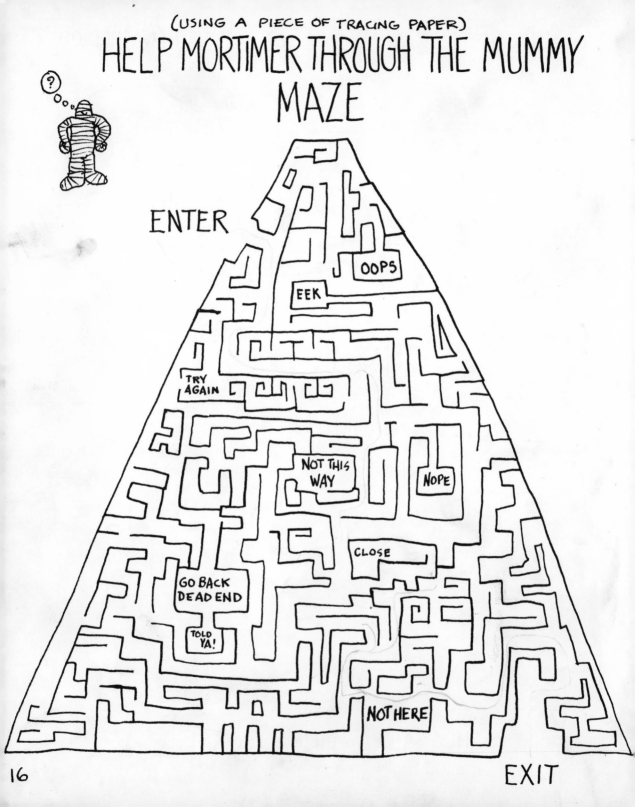

WHERE DOES A MUMMY GET A DRINK?

FROM A PHARAOH FAUCET.

WHAT'S THE DIFFERENCE BETWEEN A LOG AND A CROCODILE?

IF YOU DON'T KNOW, YOU'D BETTER NOT SWIM IN THE NILE.

WHAT DO YOU CALL A GIRL MUMMY WHO PLAYS BASEBALL?

A TOMB-BOY.

WHAT DID THE MUMMY SAY ABOUT THE BAD MOVIE?

REVENGE OF THE RETURN OF THE SON OF THE PLANET OF THE MUMMY SNATCHERS

IT SPHINX.

WHAT KIND OF MUSIC DID PHARAOHS LIKE?

ROCK AND ROLL.

WHAT KIND OF MONEY DO MUMMIES USE?

SAND DOLLARS.

EASY—TO—MAKE MUMMY

WHAT YOU WILL NEED

ONE DEAD PHARAOH
OR
AN OLD DOLL OR STUFFED ANIMAL

A ROLL OF GAUZE BANDAGE
OR
AN OLD SHEET RIPPED INTO STRIPS

SCISSORS

WHAT DID THE MUMMY SAY WHEN HE WAS UNWRAPPED?

OUT OF SIGHT, MAN.

WHY DOES MORTIMER HAVE A ROUGH TIME WITH HIS HOMEWORK?

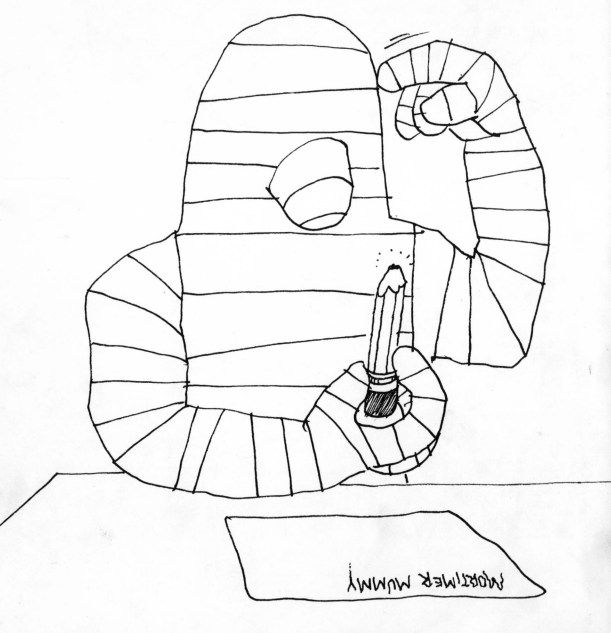

HE USES SANDPAPER.

WHAT DO YOU SAY TO A NAUGHTY MUMMY?

He wrote dirty hieroglyphics on the wall.

TUT! TUT!

DO MUMMIES HAVE GOOD EYESIGHT?

BETTER
CRYPTS
AND
GARDENS

SURE. HAVE YOU EVER SEEN A MUMMY WEARING GLASSES?

WHAT DID THE NEARSIGHTED MUMMY WEAR?

CONTACT BANDAGES.

WHY DID THE PHARAOH FIRE HIS BUILDER?

HE COULDN'T GET THE POINT.

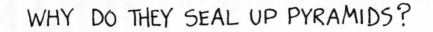

WHY DO THEY SEAL UP PYRAMIDS?

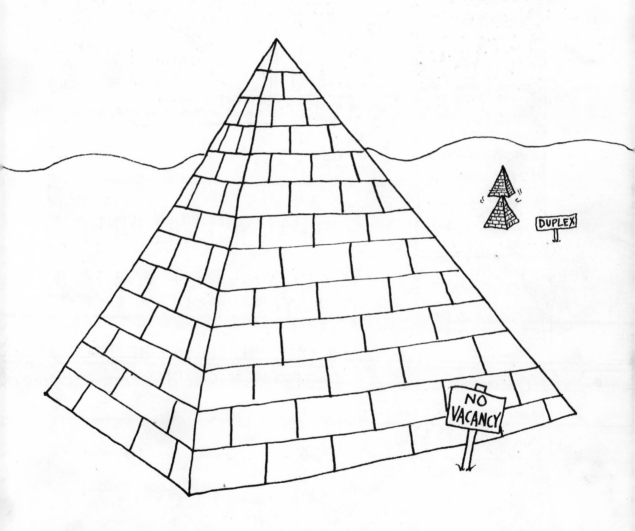

BECAUSE THE PHARAOHS ARE JUST DYING TO GET IN.

THE MUMMY

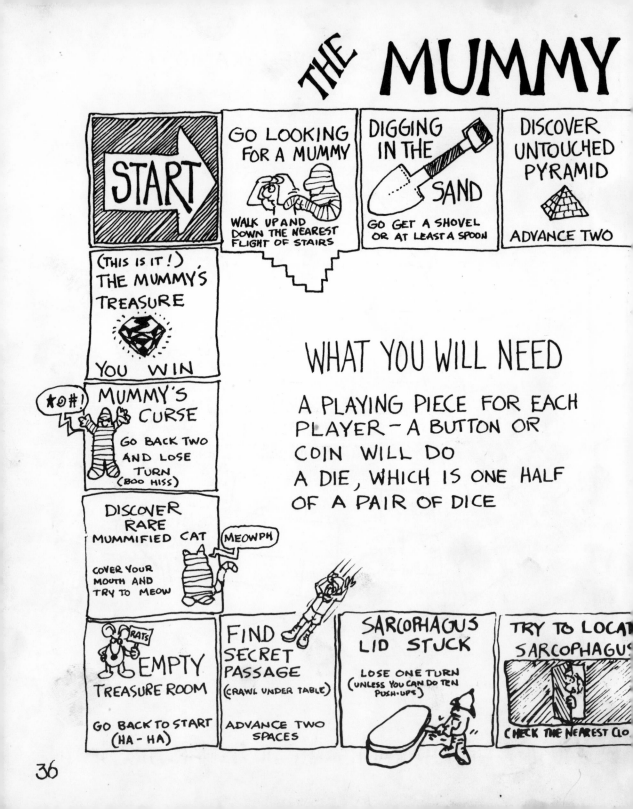

START

GO LOOKING FOR A MUMMY
WALK UP AND DOWN THE NEAREST FLIGHT OF STAIRS

DIGGING IN THE SAND
GO GET A SHOVEL OR AT LEAST A SPOON

DISCOVER UNTOUCHED PYRAMID
ADVANCE TWO

(THIS IS IT!) THE MUMMY'S TREASURE
YOU WIN

WHAT YOU WILL NEED

A PLAYING PIECE FOR EACH PLAYER — A BUTTON OR COIN WILL DO
A DIE, WHICH IS ONE HALF OF A PAIR OF DICE

★◎#!

MUMMY'S CURSE
GO BACK TWO AND LOSE TURN
(BOO HISS)

DISCOVER RARE MUMMIFIED CAT MEOWPH
COVER YOUR MOUTH AND TRY TO MEOW

RATS

EMPTY TREASURE ROOM
GO BACK TO START
(HA - HA)

FIND SECRET PASSAGE
(CRAWL UNDER TABLE)
ADVANCE TWO SPACES

SARCOPHAGUS LID STUCK
LOSE ONE TURN
(UNLESS YOU CAN DO TEN PUSH-UPS)

TRY TO LOCATE SARCOPHAGUS
CHECK THE NEAREST CLO.

'S CURSE

ACTIVATE TRAP DOOR
LOSE ONE TURN

SIT ON THE FLOOR

SEARCH FOR HIEROGLYPHICS

ON THE BOTTOMS OF EVERYONE'S SHOES

YOUR CAMEL BITES

YOU HAVE TO STAND FOR YOUR NEXT TWO TURNS (OUCH)

FIND MAP TO TREASURE
OR DRAW YOUR OWN

SAY HURRAY, JUMP UP AND DOWN THREE TIMES

DUST STORM MAKES YOU THIRSTY

HACK! COFF

GO GET A DRINK OF WATER

RULES

YOUNGEST PLAYER GOES FIRST
ROLL THE DIE AND ADVANCE
NUMBER ROLLED — PERFORM
EACH TASK — FIRST TO REACH
MUMMY'S TREASURE WINS

EGAD

LOST IN MAZE

LOSE ONE TURN

FIND GOLD MEDALLION

ANYTHING GOLD OR YELLOW WILL DO

ROLL AGAIN

FOLLOW THE MUMMY WRAPPINGS

WALK AROUND ROOM TWICE

EMPTY SAND FROM SHOES
(IN A WASTEPAPER BASKET)

GO BACK TWO

OH OH

BATTERIES GO DEAD IN THE CRYPT
(SHUT EYES FOR NEXT TURN.)

TAKE A BREAK — GO SWIMMING IN THE NILE

WHY DOESN'T SUPERMAN VISIT THE MUMMY AFTER DARK?

HE'S AFRAID OF CRYPT O NIGHT.

WHAT'S WORSE THAN BUMPING INTO A MUMMY?

BUMPING INTO TWO MUMMIES.

SURE. THEY'RE BOUND TO WIN.

WHAT'S THE DIFFERENCE BETWEEN A KANGAROO AND A MUMMY?

ONE BOUNDS AROUND; THE OTHER IS BOUND AROUND.

A BUM WRAP

PEAR A MID

A CAMEL CIGARETTE

44

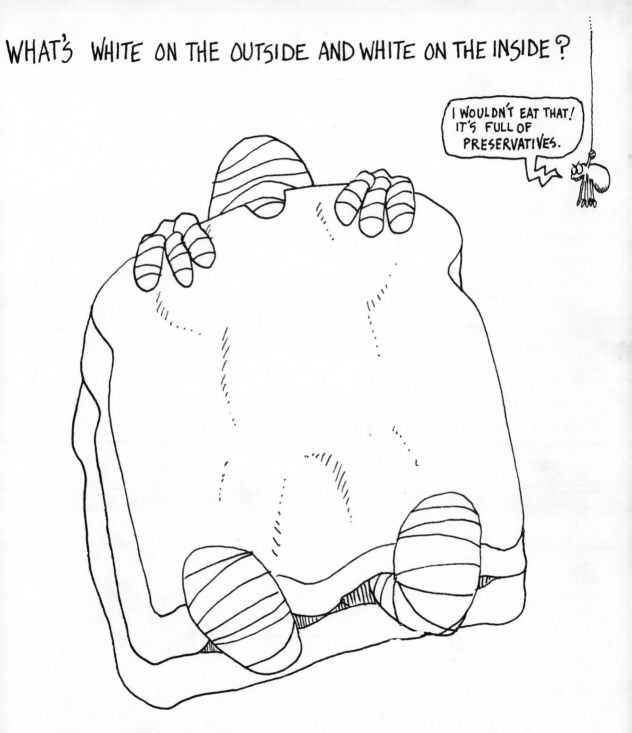

WHAT'S WHITE ON THE OUTSIDE AND WHITE ON THE INSIDE?

A MUMMY SANDWICH.

EASY TO BUILD SARCOPHAGUS
(EASIER TO BUILD THAN TO SAY)

WHAT YOU WILL NEED

A SHOE BOX WITH A LID
CLOTH OR WALL PAPER SCRAPS
SCISSORS
GLUE
MARKERS, CRAYONS, OR PAINT

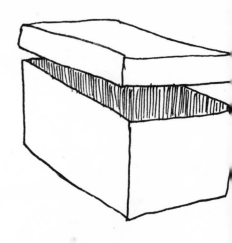

WHAT TO DO

LINE THE INSIDE OF BOX
  WITH SCRAP MATERIAL
PAINT OR COVER THE OUTSIDE
  (MAKE IT LOOK LIKE STONE OR GOLD)
        OR
DRAW A PICTURE OF A PHARAOH ON TOP

OTHER IDEAS

GLUE BUTTONS, SEQUINS,
  OR COSTUME JEWELRY TO
  THE OUTSIDE TO LOOK LIKE GEMS

WHAT BLEW UP THE MUMMY'S HOUSE?

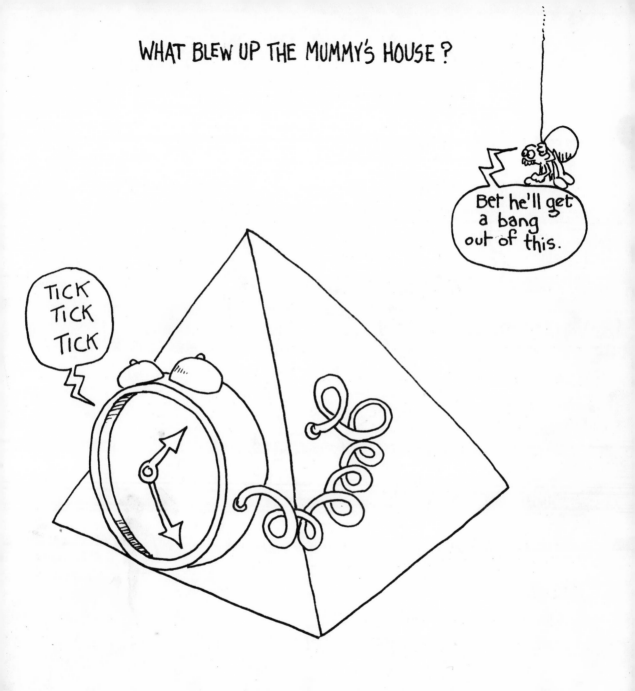

A TOMB BOMB.

WHAT DO YOU CALL A MUMMY ON FIRE?

THE LAST OF THE RED HOT MUMMIES.

HOW IS A MUMMY LIKE A CHRISTMAS PRESENT?

THEY ARE BOTH WRAPPED UP.

WHY DIDN'T THE MUMMY STAY IN JAIL?

IT WAS A BUM WRAP.

WHY DID MORTIMER PLANT A DATE TREE?

DATES ARE HARD TO GET IF YOU'RE A MUMMY.

DRAWING OF AN ASPFAULT (ASPHALT).

54

WHERE DO MUMMIES GO FOR PIZZA?

HOW MUCH DOES A MUMMY WEIGH WITHOUT ALL HIS BANDAGES?

A SKELE-TON.

WHY DON'T MUMMIES USE RULERS?

THEY PREFER TAPE MEASURES.

WHY DID THE MUMMY BLUSH?

SOMEONE WRAPPED HIM IN SCOTCH TAPE.

WHAT WOULD YOU CALL A PHARAOH'S FUNERAL?

A WRAP SESSION.

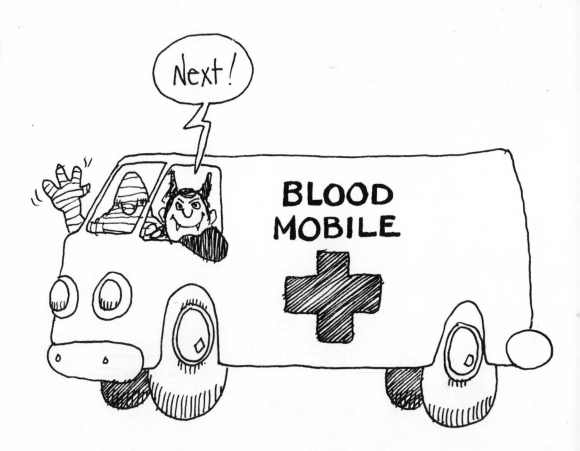

DID THE ANCIENT EGYPTIANS USE MOTORBOATS?

NAAH. EVERYBODY KNOWS THE PHAR-ROWED.

SOMETHING TO DO NEXT TIME YOU ARE
BORED

GATHER A MUMMY'S TREASURE

OLD JUNK JEWELRY
SHINY STONES
AND OTHER NEAT STUFF

PUT IT IN A BOX

WRAP THE BOX IN A PLASTIC BAG
BURY THE TREASURE

MAKE A MAP AND GIVE IT TO A FRIEND

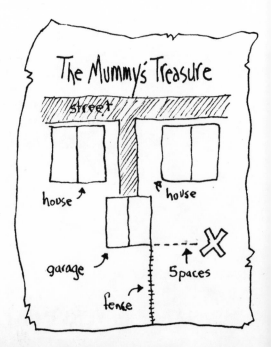

The Mummy's Treasure

street

house → ← house

garage → ← 5paces

fence →

WHAT'S A MUMMY AFTER IT'S 4,000 YEARS OLD?

4,001 YEARS OLD.

HOW CAN YOU MAKE TWO MUMMIES OUT OF ONE?

MAKE HIM SO MAD HE'S BESIDE HIMSELF.

WHAT HAPPENS WHEN A MUMMY EATS TOO MUCH?

HE GETS A TOMBIE ACHE.

WHAT WOULD YOU CALL AN ICE COLD MUMMY ON A BIKE?

A MUMMY SICLE.

WHAT DID THE MUMMY SAY WHEN THE ARCHAEOLOGIST DUG UP HIS TOMB?

WHAT KIND OF BOOKS DO MUMMIES LIKE?

MYSTERIES. THEY LOVE TO UNRAVEL THEM.

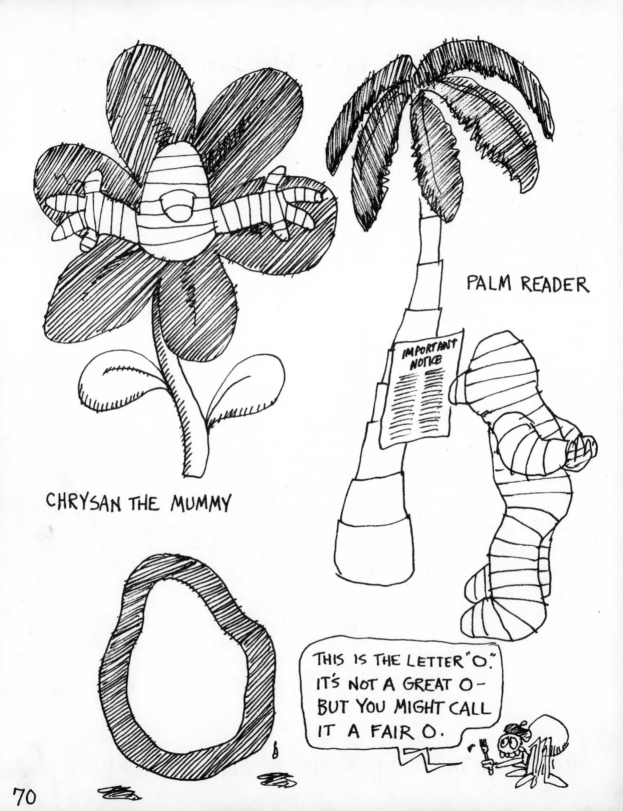

CHRYSAN THE MUMMY

PALM READER

IMPORTANT NOTICE

THIS IS THE LETTER "O."
IT'S NOT A GREAT O —
BUT YOU MIGHT CALL
IT A FAIR O.

70

ABOUT THE AUTHOR & BOOK

MY NAME IS DAVE ROSS. I LIVE NEAR SARATOGA SPRINGS, NEW YORK, IN A HOUSE THAT USED TO BE A CHICKEN COOP. I HAVE BEEN DRAWING FUNNY PICTURES AND MAKING UP JOKES SINCE I WAS FOUR YEARS OLD.

THE IDEA FOR THIS BOOK CAME FROM A LADY NAMED MAURY SOLOMON (MAURY IS AN EDITOR). SHE ALSO HELPED ME PUT THE BOOK TOGETHER.

MAURY & PUCK

MY FAMILY HELPED ME WRITE SOME OF THE RIDDLES. I TESTED ALL THE JOKES ON MY TWO SONS. YOU CAN FIND A PICTURE OF THEM ON THE COPYRIGHT PAGE.

THE CARTOONS AND LETTERING WERE FIRST SKETCHED IN PENCIL. THE COVER WAS COLORED WITH MARKERS, TEMPERA, AND ACRYLIC PAINT. THE INSIDE ART WORK WAS DONE IN FELT-TIPPED PEN. A PRINTER PUT MY DRAWINGS ON THE PAGES OF THIS BOOK.

GOING MY WAY?

EUROPE

BESIDES WRITING AND ILLUSTRATING CHILDREN'S BOOKS, I TEACH ART, MAKE SCULPTURE, AND LIKE TO TRAVEL.